From Fail to Win!
Learning from Bad Ideas

GADGETS and INVENTIONS

Neil Morris

Raintree

www.raintreepublishers.co.uk
Visit our website to find out more information about Raintree books.

To order:
☎ Phone 0845 6044371
🖷 Fax +44 (0) 1865 312263
🖳 Email myorders@raintreepublishers.co.uk

Customers from outside the UK please telephone +44 1865 312262

Raintree is an imprint of Capstone Global Library Limited, a company incorporated in England and Wales having its registered office at 7 Pilgrim Street, London, EC4V 6LB – Registered company number: 6695582

Edited by Andrew Farrow and Vaarunika Dharmapala
Designed by Richard Parker
Picture research by Mica Brancic
Originated by Capstone Global Library Ltd
Printed and bound in China by South China Printing Company Ltd

ISBN 978 1 406 21765 0 (hardback)
14 13 12 11 10
10 9 8 7 6 5 4 3 2 1

ISBN 978 1 406 21934 0 (paperback)
15 14 13 12 11
10 9 8 7 6 5 4 3 2 1

British Library Cataloguing in Publication Data
Morris, Neil.
From fail to win : learning from bad ideas.
Gadgets and inventions.
600-dc22
A full catalogue record for this book is available from the British Library.

Acknowledgements
We would like to thank the following for permission to reproduce photographs: Alamy p. **13** (© Photos 12); Corbis pp. **15** (© Bettmann), **17** (Sygma/© Eric Robert), **19 bottom** (© Reuters/Eriko Sugita), **25** (epa/Jacek Bednarczyk), **42** (© Morton Beebe); Edison National Historic Site p. **16**; Getty Images pp. **5** (George Eastman House/W. K. L. Dickson), **8** (Keystone/Alan Band/Hulton Archive/Photoshot), **10** (WireImage/Alex Henry Moore), **11** (Hulton Archive), **21**, **23** (Popperfoto/Rolls Press), **29** (AFP/Caio Leal), **31** (Hulton Archive/M.J. Rivise Patent Collection), **33 main** (Science & Society Picture Library), **37** (Hulton Archive/Fox Photos), **38** (AFP/Toshifumi Kitamura), **43** (Science & Society Picture Library); Honda news p. **19 top**; iStockphoto p. **44** (© Vitaly Shabalyn); Library of Congress p. **7**; NASA pp. **47**, **48**, **49**; Rex Features pp. **39**, **45** (Daily Mail/Bill Orchard); Science Photo Library pp. **26**, **40** (Geoff Tompkinson); Shutterstock p. **33 inset** (© stocknadia); TopFoto p. **34**.

Cover photograph of a robot playing the organ, Waseda University, Tokyo, Japan, 1985, reproduced with permission of Rex Features (Edwin Karmiol).

We would like to thank Chris Oxlade for his invaluable help in the preparation of this book.

Every effort has been made to contact copyright holders of material reproduced in this book. Any omissions will be rectified in subsequent printings if notice is given to the publisher.

Contents

Lessons learned 4

Concrete furniture 6

Picturephone 8

Smell-O-Vision 10

Talking toy 14

Household robot 18

Paper clothing 22

Vote recorder 26

Shaving device 30

Telemobiloscope 34

Internet fridge 38

Videodisc 42

Hubble Space Telescope 46

Timeline 50

Glossary 52

Find out more 54

Index 56

Any words appearing in the text in bold, **like this**,
are explained in the glossary

Lessons learned

Throughout history successful inventors have created things that never existed before. Some were huge objects or systems, others were small devices or gadgets. Individuals had the courage and **enterprise** to follow their dreams. Sometimes one development led to another. This has especially been the case since the **Industrial Revolution** of the 18th and 19th centuries.

Not all these inventions succeeded. Some failed to work properly because of a lack of technical knowledge on the part of the inventor. Others worked but were unsuccessful because there was simply no demand for them at the time. Short-term failure can, however, sometimes lead to long-term success, especially when problems are identified and overcome. This means that later inventors can learn a great deal from earlier poor or failed ideas.

World's greatest inventor?

Thomas Edison may be the greatest inventor who ever lived. He was granted 1,093 **patents** in the United States, a far greater number than any other inventor. In 1876 Edison built an industrial research laboratory at Menlo Park, New Jersey, USA. There he and his assistants began the work that led to his greatest achievements:

- a telephone transmitter that improved the invention of Alexander Graham Bell (1877)
- the **phonograph** (also called a gramophone) (1877)
- a long-lasting electric light bulb that could be used in the home (1879).

Edison always worked hard. One of his best-known sayings was, "Genius is one per cent inspiration and ninety-nine per cent perspiration." Despite his enormous success rate, Edison had his disappointments, too. Three of his failed inventions appear in this book.

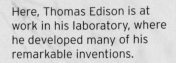

Here, Thomas Edison is at work in his laboratory, where he developed many of his remarkable inventions.

Patents

A patent protects an invention from being copied. It grants the inventor the sole right to his or her creation. However, there is nothing to say that patented inventions have to work perfectly or even be successful! For more information on patents, see page 55.

From fail to win

We have ranked the failures in this book in reverse order, from 12 to 1, ending with the failure from which we have learned the most. However, the ranking is a matter of opinion. What do you think: do you agree with the order of the book?

Daring to try

"Failure is not an option." This saying became a slogan of space exploration (see page 47). No doubt many companies would like to say this to all their employees. In fact, the saying makes little sense: failure is always possible if you dare to try something new.

Sometimes inventors are ahead of their time, so their ideas only take off later. We have examples of these kinds of ideas in this book, such as the Picturephone, Edison's vote recorder, Samuel Bligh's shaver, Christian Hülsmeyer's Telemobiloscope, and the videodisc.

Concrete furniture

Even the most successful people sometimes make mistakes. In Thomas Edison's case, there were more than a few flops. One of his biggest and most costly failures came from his belief that people would like houses and furniture made of concrete. He was ahead of his time with the idea for concrete buildings, which are commonplace today. Concrete furniture, on the other hand, has never caught on.

From iron to cement and concrete

By the 1890s Edison was designing industrial equipment for an iron-ore plant in New Jersey. When this **enterprise** failed, Edison decided to use the equipment in a different way. In 1902 he founded the Edison Portland Cement Company and successfully sold both cement and concrete. His concrete was used for the walls of the original Yankee Stadium baseball arena in New York. His company and others made too much concrete, and soon there was not enough demand. Edison looked for other ways to use the material.

The young Edison

Thomas Alva Edison was born in Milan, Ohio, USA in 1847. He found school boring, and left at the age of 12. He decided to sell newspapers and sandwiches on railway trains. When he was 16 he became an apprentice **telegraph** operator. By then he was partially deaf, but he did not allow his hearing problems to hold him back. In 1868 Edison moved to Boston, where he worked on a fire alarm system, a telegraphic printer, and applied for his first **patent**.

Houses and cabinets

Edison intended to pour his concrete into huge moulds, so that even the frame of a house would be made of one piece of concrete. He made the mistake of saying that he could make concrete houses affordable for poor people. This put potential customers off, because no one wanted to think of themselves as poor. So Edison looked at smaller items. He made a **phonograph** cabinet out of concrete, but this was not popular either. The phonograph (see page 14) was a huge success, but the cabinet was not.

The phonograph cabinet to the left of Edison is made of wood. The one to the right is concrete and was much less popular.

FAIL!

Perhaps Edison's most amazing attempt was his concrete piano. The working parts were the same as in a wooden piano, but the surrounding cabinet was made of concrete. Apparently it worked and sounded quite good, but it was a complete failure. This was probably because people saw concrete as a cold, lifeless material. They preferred wood, which they found more natural and pleasant.

What was learned?

Today concrete is one of the world's most important and useful building materials. It is fire-resistant, waterproof, and can be moulded into any shape. It can also be reinforced (made stronger) with steel. Most skyscrapers, factories, and homes stand on concrete foundations. Many buildings also have concrete frames, walls, and floors. However, concrete furniture and pianos have never been seen again.

Picturephone

The idea of a videophone – a telephone that sends and receives video images as well as sound – has been around for a long time. One of the first attempts was seen in Fritz Lang's famous futuristic film *Metropolis*, which was made in 1927. During the 1960s and 1970s, an American company invested 15 years' work and about $500 million developing a videophone system. Although it worked, the system never caught on and the idea was dropped.

Developing the videophone

The first public demonstration of a two-way videophone link took place in New York as long ago as 1930. There was little further development for another 30 years, as telecommunications companies concentrated on improving telephones and television systems separately.

Sixties system

By 1964 the American Telephone and **Telegraph** Company (AT&T) had developed its own system, called Picturephone. It was presented at the 1964 New York World's Fair. The company conducted experiments for several years, and launched a public Picturephone system in 1970.

FAIL!

As well as showing an image of the caller, the Picturephone could be used to send information. Today, we use computers and the Internet for this.

The Picturephone's black-and-white screen was 14 centimetres (5.5 inches) wide and built into a desktop unit. The system was expensive and few people took it up. According to some press reports, there were only 500 subscribers in three cities – New York, Washington, and Chicago.

What was learned?

Perhaps people were just not that interested in seeing the people they were talking to on the phone. Also, the Picturephone was difficult to use and because so few other people had them, there seemed little point in buying one. It was just one of those ideas that simply did not have a **market**.

The latest mobile phones can use built-in cameras and Universal Mobile Telecommunications System (UMTS) technology to send live video images and sound across the world. This no longer seems amazing and can be part of an overall phone package. Nevertheless, we still have to wait and see whether most people are really that interested in seeing the person they are talking to.

New developments

The development of special software applications for computers means that people can use their computer and a webcam to talk to and see others with the same application. The most popular thing about this system is that the calls are free. Yet it is still not something most people use to communicate with each other very often. It can take many years to find out whether a technology will be accepted as useful by the general public.

Smell-O-Vision

Over the years, many different gimmicks have been offered to cinema audiences. They were supposed to add thrills and excitement to the films, but unfortunately they did not always work. One of the best-known examples is the use of special red-and-green glasses to view 3-D films. The first 3-D film was shown in Los Angeles, USA in 1922, but it was not a great success. Nevertheless, 3-D has been tried many times since, and a new attempt was made with the **science fiction** film *Avatar* in 2009. The 3-D glasses they used were non-coloured and *Avatar* was an enormous hit on release.

Three-dimensional films may have struggled to be successful, but they have done better than "smelly" productions. Only one film was ever produced in Smell-O-Vision – the American thriller *Scent of Mystery* (1960) – and it was a failure. Other smelly systems have been tried since, but visual and sound gimmicks have usually fared better.

These cinema-goers are wearing special glasses to enjoy a 3-D film in 2009.

How the system worked

For each showing of *Scent of Mystery*, a series of 30 aroma containers were arranged in the right order, linked together in a belt, and wound on to a reel. The reel was attached to the film projector, and as the film was shown, markers on it would activate the Smell-O-Vision reel. Then a needle pierced one of the aroma containers, releasing a scent. Fans blew the odour through pipes to vents beneath the audience's seats.

Scent of Mystery

Scent of Mystery was made in 1960 and directed by Jack Cardiff. Odours were part of the story. In the opening scene a butterfly flutters through a grove of peach trees, which the cinema audience could smell. Later, a barrel of wine falls off a cart and smashes to pieces, releasing a strong grapey aroma of wine. At the end, the audience could recognize the killer by the smell of his smoking pipe.

Inventor Hans Laube (right) shows the smell system to *Scent of Mystery* producer Mike Todd.

Why the system failed

Scent of Mystery opened in cinemas in New York, Los Angeles, and Chicago, but unfortunately Smell-O-Vision did not always work properly. Some reviewers said that the aromas made a hissing noise under the seats, and filmgoers in the balcony complained that the smells reached them some time after the action on the screen.

"First they moved (1895)! Then they talked (1927)! Now they smell!"

From an advertisement for *Scent of Mystery*

Odour problems

Some viewers said the odours were too faint, which caused people to sniff loudly and annoy the rest of the audience. One comedian joked that he could not smell any of the aromatic effects because he had a cold. It was reported that the technical problems were sorted out after early screenings, but the poor response soon meant the end of Smell-O-Vision. The film was eventually re-released without odours as *Holiday in Spain*.

What has been learned?

Up until now, vision–smell combination systems have not succeeded. Perhaps that will change in the digital age. In 2001 a computer company based in California developed an electronic device that could be connected to a personal computer to produce odours. Called the iSmell Personal Scent Synthesizer, it was designed to give off a smell when a user visited a website or opened an email with an odour encoded in it. The iSmell had 128 odours, which could be mixed to make other smells. Unfortunately the company went out of business, but many other film and computer companies have been working on developing smell technology. Have they learned from the failures of the past?

Today and tomorrow

In 2006 an application was made to the US **Patent** Office for a "digital scent movie projector with sound channel". According to the applicant, a sense-of-smell signal can be programmed into digital movies, so that the viewer can enjoy the triple effect of sight, sound, and smell. The following year, a computer software company released its own smell system, which it claimed can be used for aromatherapy, to make people feel better by inhaling aromas. Perhaps in the future, smells over the Internet will succeed where smells in the cinema failed.

Polyester

Made in 1981, the American comedy film *Polyester* used a different smell system called Odorama. This involved giving "scratch-and-sniff" cards to the audience when they bought their tickets. The cards had spots numbered 1 to 10, and when a number appeared on the screen, viewers scratched and sniffed that spot.

Scents included a bouquet of flowers, grass, and freshly made pizza. At one point in the film, a joke was played on the audience. When they scratched the number for fresh flowers, they received a nasty whiff of sweaty shoes.

This is the scratch-and-sniff card used for the film *Polyester*.

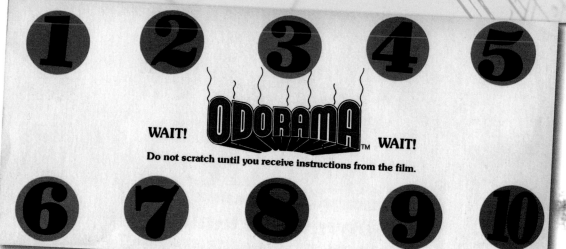

WAIT! ODORAMA™ WAIT!
Do not scratch until you receive instructions from the film.

Edison had great success with his **phonograph**, a machine in which a needle picked up sounds from a revolving cylinder or disc and played them though a loudspeaker. The first words Edison recorded, in 1877, were "Mary had a little lamb". He soon became known as the Wizard of Menlo Park (where his laboratory was), but the truth is that the new invention was a bit of a curiosity. Nobody knew exactly what to do with it. Edison himself thought it would be very useful as a dictating machine. Music discs, called gramophone records, were not released until 1887, and it was another 25 years before Edison himself started making recorded discs.

Nursery rhymes

Perhaps it was significant that Edison's first ever recording was a nursery rhyme. In the same year, 1877, he decided that a good use for his new invention would be to make dolls talk. He bought dolls' heads from Germany and made his own doll. It was 56 centimetres (22 inches) tall, with a porcelain head, metal body, and wooden arms and legs. Inside the body, Edison put a tiny 18-centimetre (7-inch) tall phonograph, which worked by playing a wax cylinder with a steel needle. The phonograph had no motor, so the child who owned the doll had to turn a key by hand to hear words "spoken" by the doll. These were nursery rhymes, such as *Jack and Jill*, *Little Bo Peep*, and *Little Jack Horner*.

What went wrong?

There were several problems with Edison's talking doll. The sound quality was poor, and even Edison admitted that "the voices of the little monsters were exceedingly unpleasant to hear". Also, they were not cheap. Each doll cost US$10 with a simple dress, and up to US$25 with more interesting clothes. This was a great deal of money in those days.

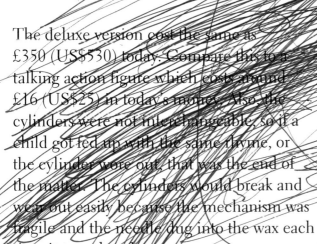

1   2

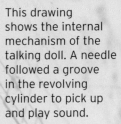

This drawing shows the internal mechanism of the talking doll. A needle followed a groove in the revolving cylinder to pick up and play sound.

The deluxe version cost the same as £350 (US$530) today. Compare this to a talking action figure which costs around £16 (US$25) in today's money. Also, the cylinders were not interchangeable, so if a child got fed up with the same rhyme, or the cylinder wore out, that was the end of the matter. The cylinders would break and wear out easily because the mechanism was fragile and the needle dug into the wax each time it was played.

"A great corporation has been organized in New York … [talking dolls] will repeat any sound, just as a phonograph does, so look out for all sorts of mimicry from toys. Millions will be manufactured and toydom will be revolutionized."

Oroville Mercury newspaper, California, around 1890

FAIL!

The talking doll must have amazed children at the time, but the sound quality was scratchy and the words were difficult to understand.

A failure

Unfortunately, forecasts of success were wrong. The dolls were on sale for only a few weeks in New York in 1890, and unhappy customers returned many of those that were sold. Edison's company made at least 2,500 dolls, but fewer than 500 were bought. Also, there was a problem with the **patent** for wax recordings, which Edison held only for dictating machines. He may have had to withdraw the doll anyway. His company took the phonographs out of the unsold and returned dolls, and then sold them off cheaply.

What was learned?

One of the lessons learned was that customers are not happy to pay for novelties that do not work properly. In fact, mechanical audio toys never really worked well, partly because they were never strong enough to withstand the rough treatment handed out by young children. This changed a century later, when toy manufacturers started putting electronic microchips into their toys. These are more reliable because they have no moving parts.

Microchips replace the phonograph, controlling the playing of recordings and even the movement of the toy. Instead of human muscle power driving the mechanism, batteries power the electronic device.

WIN!

These characters from the 1995 film *Toy Story*, Sheriff Woody (left) and Buzz Lightyear, are talking action toys. Animator John Lasseter is shaking their hands.

The Kinetophone

In 1894 Edison and his **collaborator** William Dickson introduced the Kinetoscope. This was a device that showed moving pictures through a viewer. Then Edison had the idea that he could use his phonograph technology to add sound to the Kinetoscope. In 1895 he started selling the Kinetophone. This had earphones connected to it, so that background music and other sounds could accompany the pictures.

The problem was that the sounds did not fit the pictures exactly, and the Kinetophone was not a success. The future lay with film projection. When sounds were recorded on to the film itself, people could hear music and voices at the right places. Film projection was introduced by Edison and others in 1896 and sound was first added in 1900.

Household robot

The term *robot* comes from a Czech word meaning "forced labour". It was first used in a play in 1921, and ever since, people have dreamed of having household tasks and chores done for them by mechanical devices that operate automatically. Many **science fiction** novels have featured domestic robots, and many people assumed that robots would be doing housework by the year 2000 at the latest. This did not happen, despite many attempts being made. Could it happen in the future?

Medieval robots

Long before the word *robot* was used, scientists and inventors were thinking about making **automata**, machines that could perform functions on their own according to a set of coded instructions. Around 800 years ago the Islamic scholar Al-Jazari created a **humanoid** automaton that used the power of flowing water to serve drinks. Then, in 1495, the famous scientist, artist, and inventor Leonardo da Vinci sketched designs for a mechanical automaton dressed in armour. We do not know whether Leonardo built a working model. In recent years experts have made "Leonardo's robot", and claim that it works perfectly.

Modern robots

Between 1986 and 1993 the Honda Motor Company developed seven walking robots, called E0 to E6. Each one had a pair of legs and a cube-shaped body. The developers concentrated on improving the robots' walking, so that they could climb stairs and cope with uneven surfaces.

"Although robots have computers for brains and they can be very powerful, it will be a long time before they can do all the things people can do very easily."

From *The New Book of Knowledge* encyclopedia (Grolier, 1985 edition)

This was an expert opinion expressed in 1985. In fact, the science of robotics has probably developed faster than expected. Even so, robots still have a long way to go before they can perform tasks the way humans can.

Next they added arms and a head and, between 1993 and 1997, developed P1, P2, and P3. Honda called these "the world's first self-regulating two-legged humanoid walking robots". They could walk steadily at 2 kilometres (1.24 miles) per hour. They led to a robot called ASIMO (standing for **A**dvanced **S**tep in **I**nnovative **Mo**bility) in 2000. According to Honda, ASIMO can run at 6 kilometres (3.72 miles) per hour, walk on uneven slopes and surfaces, turn smoothly, climb stairs, and reach for and grasp objects. It can also understand and respond to simple voice commands, recognize the faces of a small number of people, use its camera eyes to map its environment and register stationary objects, and avoid moving obstacles as it moves through its environment.

ASIMO has good balance and walking skills. It stands 1 m 20 cm tall (almost 4 ft).

What has been learned?

Honda was so convinced of ASIMO's abilities that they gave it a job as a receptionist in one of their Japanese offices in 2006. They say it was able to guide guests to a meeting room, serve coffee on a tray, and push a cart with a load of up to 10 kilograms (22 pounds). Despite these successes, robots will have to be much more efficient and do many more things before they can be useful in the home. At the moment they would also be extremely expensive. This means that they are not such a great idea, because wealthy people can hire a much better device to do their cleaning and other household jobs – a human being. Human cleaners can do many different things at once, as well as deciding what needs to be done next.

Robotic future?

"[In] the future, ASIMO may serve as another set of eyes, ears, hands, and legs for all kinds of people in need. Someday ASIMO might help with important tasks like assisting the elderly or a person confined to a bed or a wheelchair. ASIMO might also perform certain tasks that are dangerous to humans, such as fighting fires or cleaning up toxic spills."

Honda website
2010

What about a pet robot?

In 1999 another Japanese company, Sony Corporation, launched a robotic dog called AIBO (the Artificial Intelligence Robot). Sony called AIBO an entertainment robot and advertised it as "your artificial, intelligent friend". Updated versions were launched in 2001 and 2003, but in 2006 the company announced that it was closing its Robotics Division and ending production of AIBO.

The canine robot could walk, see its environment through a camera, and recognize some spoken commands. Most importantly, it could learn things from its owners, who could feel that they were bringing the robot up from puppy to adult dog. An AIBO cost about US$2000, and more than 150,000 were sold over 7 years. However, the costs of production were enormous and though many fans were disappointed when AIBO was withdrawn, there was no great call for a replacement.

FAIL!

This AIBO is one of the original models launched in 1999.

Paper clothing

You might think the idea of paper clothes seems ridiculous. You wouldn't be able to wear them in the rain, they would easily tear, and surely they would be uncomfortable? Despite all these disadvantages, there was a time during the 1960s when **disposable** paper clothes looked like they were becoming a huge success. One particular paper dress designed and manufactured in the United States did well for a while. The craze did not last long, even though many predicted that paper underwear was the future. Nearly 50 years later, there is still interest in disposable clothing, but every attempt to sell the idea as a fashion item seems doomed to failure.

Short-lived dresses

By the 1960s the Scott Paper Company, with factories in Wisconsin, USA, had been manufacturing toilet paper, paper towels, and napkins for many years. Then in 1966 the company launched two styles of dress to promote a new range of paper products. One of the "Paper-Caper" dresses had a black-and-white pop art pattern, and the other had a colourful paisley design. They both came in four different sizes and sold for $1.25 (80 pence) each, the same as $8.25 (£5.40) today. People who bought a dress received money-off coupons for Scott's other paper products. In fact, the dresses were not 100 per cent pure paper: they were strengthened by the inclusion of 7 per cent rayon, a **synthetic** textile fibre.

The care label on Scott Paper-Caper dresses said:
"Important: Your Paper-Caper is fire resistant, but washing, dry cleaning, or soaking will make the fabric dangerously **flammable** when dry."

This paper dress was created in 1967 by the famous fashion designer Paco Rabanne. Designers liked the idea, but buyers were not so keen.

Paper demand?

Orders for half a million dresses poured in. Perhaps this was largely because the dresses were so cheap and the extra coupons made buying them even more attractive. The paper company did not want to become a fashion company, so they quickly ended their campaign. Other companies saw an opportunity to step into the gap in the **market**. A shampoo manufacturer offered stylish paper miniskirts, and an Indian airline produced a paper sari.

"In terms of how much pow you get for your pennies, the paper dress is the ultimate smart-money fashion. And the news in the paper is this: surprisingly pretty prints, clever new shapes that would do credit to an origami expert. (Surprisingly long life too: as many as 12 outings)."

Mademoiselle magazine
June 1967

Disposable elegance

In 1967 the American fashion magazine *Look* featured dresses made of gold and silver metallic paper. This seemed a good idea at the time, and advertisers thought that disposable clothing would appeal to rebellious young people, whose parents were more interested in things that lasted. Some people even thought that paper clothes would eventually be sold in tear-off rolls at very cheap prices.

They were wrong. At this time the **hippie** lifestyle was becoming popular in America and Europe, and hippies disliked **consumerism** and especially waste. Hippies were concerned about the environment, and to them cheap textiles that lasted and could be passed on were much more interesting. They did not take to disposable paper underwear, which seemed like a wonderful idea to business executives.

What was learned?

Fashionable paper clothing failed in the 1960s and has only been seen since as a gimmick. However, experience has shown that paper can be a very useful material for other kinds of single-use clothing. It is used, for example, in hospitals and factories, when an item is expected to be worn only once for reasons of **hygiene**. Perhaps the biggest use is in babies' nappies. The disposable paper kind took over from cloth nappies in the 1980s and now dominates the market. Parents find them much more convenient, because they do not need to be washed. However, many people feel they are wasteful and harmful to the environment.

This dress, made from paper cups, was designed by a fashion student in 2009.

Electric clothes

In 2008 researchers at the Georgia Institute of Technology in the United States announced they were developing a shirt made of a material that could produce electricity. It works by covering textile fibres, such as cotton, with tiny wires made of zinc oxide. When the wires rub together as the wearer moves, they produce a small amount of electricity. This would be enough to power a mobile phone or an MP3 player. However, zinc oxide is affected by water, so power production could stop when the shirt is washed. The researchers say they are working on this problem, but perhaps the idea is heading for failure.

Project Runway

In September 2009, the US television series *Project Runway*, which focuses on fashion design, broadcast a programme on paper clothes. Designers were asked to make an outfit out of newspaper as an "alternative material", and they chose dresses and coats. The results were impressive, and the audience seemed to like them. Two months later, *Vogue* magazine ran a feature on making fashionable outfits from paper bags. Perhaps paper clothes will make a comeback after all.

Vote recorder

In 1868 Thomas Edison was working as a **telegraph** operator in Boston, USA. He had many ideas for telegraphic inventions. His design for an electrographic vote recorder became his first **patent** application. The device worked well, but when he presented it to the US Congress (which makes the nation's laws), it was turned down. Far from being put off by this failure, Edison realized that he must concentrate on devices that had a known use. As he himself said, "The vote recorder got no further than the Patent Office. But, at any rate, it had brought me to the point of giving up practical telegraphy and making invention my business."

A new system

At that time members of the House of Representatives (the lower house of the US Congress), usually voted by saying "aye" or "nay". Edison assumed that representatives would be interested in making the system of voting simpler and faster. He also discovered that the Washington city council and New York state **legislature** were considering introducing vote recorders, so he thought he should move fast. His invention allowed each voter to press a switch for "yes" or "no", and the votes appeared automatically at the **Speaker's** desk.

Thomas Edison's vote recorder was a simple device that worked well.

Presenting the idea

A telegrapher colleague of Edison's, Dewitt C. Roberts, put up $100 to help develop a **prototype** machine, and they applied for a patent in October 1868. Eight months later, the patent was granted. They then took the prototype machine to Washington, to present it to a committee of Congress. This was where everything went wrong.

Edison thought that Congress would be impressed by the speed, but this is exactly what they disliked. It turned out that the slow pace of roll-call voting was used by representatives to make long speeches at the same time, trying to convince others to change their vote. This tactic was known as filibustering, and House members were used to it and liked it.

Letters patent no. 90,646

"The object of my invention is to produce an apparatus which records and registers in an instant, and with great accuracy, the votes of legislative bodies, thus avoiding loss of valuable time consumed in counting and registering the votes and names."

Thomas Edison
1 June 1869

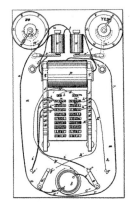

T. A. EDISON.
Electric Vote-Recorder.

No. 90,646.

Patented June 1, 1869.

Witnesses.

Inventor.

This is how Thomas Edison described the presentation.

"We got hold of the right man to get the machine adopted, and I enthusiastically set forth its merits to him. Just imagine my feelings when … he exclaimed: 'Young man, that won't do at all! … Your invention would destroy the only hope the minority have of influencing legislation. … and as the ruling majority always know that it may some day become a minority, they will be as much averse to any change as their opponents.'"

What was learned?

Edison's vote-recorder was a failure, but it led to success in two different ways. Firstly, it convinced Edison that he could invent devices that worked – but they had to be things that people wanted, not just clever ideas. Secondly, it led to other developments that eventually introduced electrical vote recorders.

The next proposal for automated voting was put to Congress in 1886. Once again the Committee turned it down. This situation was repeated many times until, at last, use of an electronic voting system was authorized in the United States in 1970. This finally showed that there was nothing fundamentally wrong with Edison's original idea. It was just that he was in the wrong place at the wrong time.

How representatives vote today

The House of Representatives has 435 voting members. They vote at one of the boxes located throughout the chamber. They insert a small plastic card that contains a magnetic identification strip. Then they press one of three buttons. "Yea" means yes, to agree with the bill, "Nay" means no, to disagree, and "Present" simply shows that they are present at the vote.

British system

The British House of Commons still has the old-fashioned system. Votes are called divisions, because members of parliament divide into two areas called the "Aye" and "No" lobbies. The MPs' names are recorded there by clerks and counted by tellers.

E-elections

Today computer technology makes it possible to vote electronically. The first fully electronic general elections were held in Brazil in 2000. Voters go to special stations to use a portable electronic voting machine, which has batteries as a back-up in case of a power failure. Voters press several keys to vote, and sometimes a paper printout of the vote is also produced.

Critics have suggested that it might be possible for fraudsters to abuse the system, but there have not been any major problems since e-voting was introduced.

This voting machine was used in the 2006 presidential elections in Brazil.

Shaving device

At the end of the 19th century, inventors and razor manufacturers were starting to develop new kinds of shavers. The founder of the Gillette Safety Razor Company, King Camp Gillette, was working on a new safety razor with replaceable steel blades. At the same time, a less well-known inventor named Samuel Bligh, of Pennsylvania, USA, was working on a very different shaving device. Unlike the Gillette version, the Bligh model required no soap and water. You might think this was a big advantage, but success went to the wet razor. While Bligh failed to get his shaver off the ground at all, Gillette went on to sell 70 million safety razors in 1915.

Developing a good shave

The forerunner of the modern safety razor was a steel blade with a guard along one edge. This was developed in Sheffield, England, in 1828. It was much more popular than the old straight razor, known for good reason as the cutthroat, but Bligh thought he could invent a mechanical device that would not need soap and water.

In August 1899 Bligh filed a **patent** application for his new dry shaving device. Instead of a sharp blade, the shaver had a roller covered in emery paper. Emery is a form of the mineral corundum that can be ground into tiny pieces, attached to paper or board, and used as an abrasive for grinding, smoothing, and polishing things. Emery board, for example, is used for filing fingernails. Bligh's emery roller was meant to turn fast and wear or rub the stubble on a man's face away.

His device had to be attached to some kind of driving force. In his patent application, it was attached to the treadle of a sewing machine, which the shaving man operated with his feet.

Letters patent no. 646,065

"The present invention has for its object to provide a device for shaving by abrasion, to take the place of the usual razor or other like cutting implement. … The abrading surface of the roller is held in contact with the face of the user and … the roller moved over the face as the beard is worn away, the device to be used on a perfectly dry face, no soap or water being used."

Samuel Bligh
27 March 1900

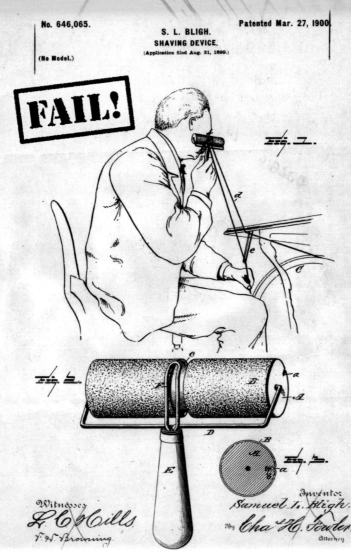

Problems

Bligh's shaving device failed for several reasons. Firstly, it must have given a very uncomfortable or even painful "shave", which was more like a scrape or a grind. It would certainly have exfoliated the face, removing the top layer of skin. It must also have been very difficult to use, since it would not be easy to attach to a "suitable driving wheel". Furthermore, it was not portable, or even usable in the bathroom, because of the need for a driving wheel. Gillette's safety razor, on the other hand, was easily portable. In fact, in 1918 Gillette provided all American soldiers with a razor set, paid for by the US government.

Samuel Bligh

Samuel Bligh was an experienced inventor, although his creations had not had any great success. Between 1895 and 1900 he obtained patents for an axle-nut wrench, a broom-holder, cheese-cutter, corn-husker, and fire-kindler.

What was learned?

Razor inventors were aware that they had to solve the problem of mechanical or electrical power. All the new developments took place in the United States. In 1910 Willis Shockey took out a patent on his wind-up razor, with a revolving wheel that the user wound up by hand.

This form of power was more practical than Bligh's, but the next step was even better. In the 1920s a retired US Army colonel named Jacob Schick developed an electric shaver. However, he had to wait until 1928 to find an electric motor small enough to fit inside a hand-held device that was powerful enough to drive blades that gripped and cut a man's beard. This was the real breakthrough, and the Schick dry shaver was hugely successful. Later electric shavers manufactured by Remington, Philips, and others were even smaller than Schick's and were powered by batteries.

Wet versus dry

While electric shavers gained a large share of the **market**, many men still prefer a wet shave with soap and water. They believe this gives a closer shave and is better for their face. Advertising has convinced many of this, and modern safety razors have multiple blades "for an even closer shave". Both modern alternatives give a much better shave than Bligh's abrasive approach.

This Schick electric shaver dates from 1934.

Telemobiloscope No.4

On 9 June 1904 a young German engineer named Christian Hülsmeyer demonstrated his new invention to representatives of international shipping companies. Hülsmeyer's invention was an anti-collision device for shipping called the Telemobiloscope. It worked well in the demonstration. However, as we shall see, the spectators showed little interest and the invention failed. Looking back more than a hundred years later, we can see that the unsuccessful Telemobiloscope was an early form of one of the most important inventions of the 20th century – **radar**.

Christian Hülsmeyer is pictured here with his invention. He called it the Telemobiloscope, which means "far-off movement observing instrument".

Building on Hertz

Around 1887 the German physicist Heinrich Hertz discovered electromagnetic waves. He became the first person to transmit radio waves. His discoveries opened the way for the development of radio, radar, and television. The young Hülsmeyer was particularly interested in Hertz's findings and his studies led him to experiment with the practical uses of radio waves.

Hülsmeyer realized that radio waves bounced off metal objects and could be used to determine the presence of objects even when they could not be seen or heard. He built a device that contained a radio transmitter and receiver side by side. The transmitter sent out a signal, which bounced back to the receiver if it struck an object. The original Telemobiloscope could do this up to a range of 3 to 5 kilometres (1.8 to 3 miles). Later models increased the range to 10 kilometres (6.2 miles) and showed the exact distance of the object. Hülsmeyer thought this would be particularly useful for shipping and railways.

Who's Who: Christian Hülsmeyer (1881–1957)

"An electrical engineer who is regarded as the inventor of the principle of radar. In 1904 he created the **prototype** of the modern radar device with his Telemobiloscope, which was rediscovered three decades later and redeveloped on an international scale."

German *Who's Who*
2010

"Christian Hülsmeyer was the first to demonstrate and **patent** the core of the principle of radar, namely to detect distant objects by receiving reflected electromagnetic waves."

Joachim Ender,
Fraunhofer Institute for
High Frequency Physics
and Radar Techniques,
Germany,
2004

This early sketch shows how the Telemobiloscope worked.

Why did it fail?

Hülsmeyer gave two successful demonstrations of his invention in 1904, the first on the River Rhine in Cologne, Germany, and the second in Rotterdam, in the Netherlands. Naval observers were impressed, but they could not really see any need for the invention. A German naval officer said that a ship's siren, which made a loud noise when steam was forced through it, could carry further than the Telemobiloscope, gave sufficient warning, and made the new invention unnecessary. Perhaps they did not realize that the new technology worked in all weather conditions and was independent of sight or sound. Aircraft were then very new, so no one realized the system's usefulness for flight. Hülsmeyer went on to work in other scientific areas and took out 180 different patents.

What was learned?

During the 1930s scientists working in different countries rediscovered radar. The development of long-range bomber planes made the new research especially important, as different nations looked for ways of detecting the approach of enemy aircraft. In Germany, Rudolf Kühnold, head of the German Naval Signals Department, successfully demonstrated his radar device in 1934.

The following year, Scottish engineer Robert Watson-Watt headed a research team for the British government, looking into what they called radio detection-finding (RDF). Watson-Watt refined techniques that detected aircraft up to a distance of 140 kilometres (90 miles) away. In 1936 scientists at the US Naval Research Laboratory in Washington, DC successfully tested a system that tracked aircraft at a distance of 40 kilometres (24.8 miles) away.

The beginning of World War II in 1939 encouraged all countries to improve their radar systems. By the end of the war in 1945, radar had improved and anti-radar systems were also being used.

Robert Watson-Watt experimented with radio transmitters and kites in 1931. This led to the development of radar.

Hülsmeyer and Watson-Watt

Who invented radar? Reference books agree that many different scientists were involved. Most make mention of both Christian Hülsmeyer and Robert Watson-Watt, though there was a great difference between them. Hülsmeyer's Telemobiloscope failed to make any impact at the time, while Watson-Watt's RDF was so successful that he was knighted for his contribution to the **Allies** in World War II.

Hülsmeyer had been forgotten, but in 1948 a German historian wrote an article about his early work. In 1953 both Hülsmeyer and Watson-Watt were invited to a conference on radar in Frankfurt, Germany. They met as fellow scientists and inventors who had both been involved in the development of radar.

Internet fridge

At the turn of the present century, manufacturers of fridges and other "white goods" turned to the Internet. They were looking for ways to improve their products and increase their profits. Surely people would be interested in a smart fridge that could automatically order a carton of milk when stocks were running low? The answer was a resounding "no", and so far the Internet-connected fridge has been a flop. People are quite happy to write their own shopping list and attach it to the fridge with a magnet. They might then use the Internet to order their groceries online, but they can do that from their laptop. Of course things might change in the future, and the present kitchen failures might turn into winners.

Developing the electronic home

Since the birth of the home computer in the 1980s, many people have predicted that computer-controlled electronics would take over in the home. From the comfort of your sofa, you would be able to lock doors, close curtains, activate the home cinema and other entertainment consoles, and even order dinner.

This early Internet fridge was shown at an exhibition in Japan in 1998.

Even better, you would be able to get your computer to do many of these things automatically, at a particular time of day, according to the weather, and so on. People thought that one of the best places to start on this revolution was in the kitchen.

In the 1990s inventors and manufacturers started work on making kitchen appliances "smarter", or more electronically intelligent. Much development was based on the fact that people lead such busy lives that they no longer have time to think about ordering food or shopping. This is where the use of the Internet came in. For example, a manufacturer developed a "net-enabled" microwave oven that allowed busy office workers to use the Internet to send cooking instructions and have dinner cooked and waiting for them when they got home from work.

What can a fridge do?

In the early 2000s manufacturers built as many electronic capabilities as they could into their products. For the latest state-of-the-art fridge, they added a computer screen in the door and connected the computer to the Internet. Now the user could set the computer to track the amount of certain types of food and flag them up for re-ordering. At the same time, the computer could provide shopping lists, recipes, and other helpful data. The fridge might also be useful for surfing the Internet in the kitchen, as well as sending and checking emails.

Large Internet fridges seemed like a good idea to manufacturers looking for a new sales angle.

What has been learned?

There are several reasons why the smart fridge has been a failure. Firstly, it was more expensive than other fridges, and buyers already had their own computers and Internet connections. Experts call this a classic case of over-engineering, because the capabilities offered were not really wanted. People still like writing shopping lists and being in charge of groceries themselves. Online shopping is already successful, but there was no need to add the fridge to this. There was another problem. Everyone knows that modern computers have a short lifetime of just a few years before both the hardware and software are out of date, or at least need upgrading.

High-tech electronics help the food industry in many new ways. The sensors in this electronic nose detect, measure, and analyse smells. This helps maintain quality control for food and drink.

However, consumers expect a fridge to last at least ten years before they invest in a new model. So the smart part of the fridge would be outmoded long before the traditional part. Finally, the development of the electronic kitchen has been held back by the fact that the various appliances from different manufacturers are not always compatible with each other.

Touch-screen shopping

In 2009 a supermarket chain introduced touch-screen shopping. The idea is that by using their computer programme, a family can keep all its food-shopping needs in one place. They can plan meals by dragging products, using the touch screen, into a particular day in their shopping calendar. They can build up a favourites list and download recipes from celebrity cooks and follow step-by-step instructions. All this at the touch of a screen. Will this new online system be more successful than the Internet fridge?

The paperless office

The Internet fridge has not been the only failure in the modern electronic world. For some years business experts have been talking about a "paperless office". They thought that computers and other electronic equipment would do away with paper.

In fact, figures show that we use more paper than ever before, especially in printers connected to computers, at home as well as in the office. In the world's richest countries, the average person consumes 152 kilograms (335 pounds) of paper every year.

Perhaps this will change? Many banks and companies now offer their customers online statements and bills, so that they use less paper. This may be the beginning of a new trend.

The videodisc was a circular plastic disc that held moving picture and sound information that was read by a **laser**. In the 1970s many experts in entertainment and education believed that this was going to become a successful format, taking over from moving film and long-playing (LP) records all in one. Yet the videodisc failed and, to the experts' surprise, was beaten by a different system – the videocassette – that many thought was inferior. Today both systems are out of date.

"Video recording technology is changing rapidly. The latest developments of today may well seem obsolete and even primitive in another decade."

The New Book of Knowledge encyclopedia, 1985

The videodisc was invented in 1958, but was not improved until the late 1960s. In 1972 the electronics giant Philips launched its own version (pictured).

Developing video technology

In the 1960s many electronics companies were looking for new ways to move on from film and television. Film cameras and projectors were expensive, cumbersome, and difficult to operate for home users. At the same time, people wanted to be able to play films and television programmes when it suited them. There was a **market** in schools for a good, simple system for playing visual material. The videodisc seemed ideal.

How did it work?

The videodisc was a plastic disc measuring 30 centimetres (12 inches) across. Signals were recorded on the master disc by a high-power laser as a sequence of coded holes. When the disc was played, the signals were read by a laser that was focused by a lens. Variations in the amount of light reflected from the disc were sensed by the laser, and the light signals were then turned into video and audio signals to be seen and heard on a television. The function of the videodisc was very similar to the later compact disc (CD) and DVD.

What went wrong?

There were two main problems with the videodisc. The first was the high cost of the player. The second problem was competition from a totally different system, the videocassette. The videocassette contained videotape inside a plastic case. The videodisc had higher-quality sound and vision, but the videocassette players were less expensive and had one enormous advantage. They could be used to record television programmes. This meant that viewers could use them to watch programmes at times that suited them. This was a very popular feature. At peak viewing times in the evening, viewers could watch one programme live and record another on a different channel at the same time.

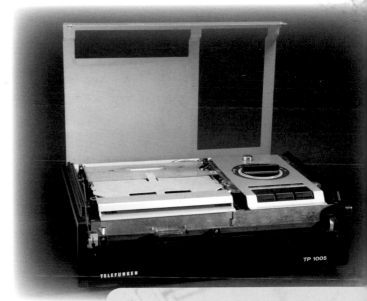

A special player and television were needed to play videodiscs. This player was made in about 1975.

Video versions

Videocassette recorders (VCRs) first came out in 1971, and became very popular by 1975–76. At that time there were two different systems from Japanese electronics giants, Sony's Betamax and JVC's VHS (Video Home System). VHS went on to win the battle of the formats, as well as completely overshadowing the videodisc. The lesson seemed to be that consumers care more about usefulness than quality.

What was learned?

In the late 1990s a new type of disc called a DVD, short for **D**igital **V**ideodisc or **D**igital **V**ersatile **D**isc, took over from the videocassette. The DVD is very similar to the earlier videodisc, only smaller. Despite this similarity, DVDs became popular while the videodisc failed to take off. This happened even though it was many years before DVD players were able to record television programmes the way videocassette recorders could. In recent years, this problem has been overcome and digital recorders, which are hard discs contained inside a box connected to the television, are widely available. Twenty-five years on from the encyclopedia prediction quoted on page 42, the same is still true: "The latest developments of today may well seem obsolete and even primitive in another decade."

DVD players, such as this one, took over from videocassette recorders.

Polavision

In 1977 the company that made Polaroid instant cameras launched an instant movie system called Polavision. Polavision worked on the same principle as Polaroid photographs, which developed within seconds of being taken.

The system was not a success, and was completely killed off in the 1980s and 1990s when small video cameras came out. You could watch your own movies from these via a VCR, which once again won out. Since then, digital cameras and mobile phones have been given video capabilities.

Polavision films had to be watched using a special viewer (pictured) or by being projected on to a screen.

Hubble Space Telescope

The Hubble Space Telescope (HST) is an **astronomical** instrument that orbits Earth. It was launched by an American space shuttle in 1990 to provide sharper, more detailed views of the universe than any Earth-based telescope. Despite billions of dollars spent on development and a successful space launch, the HST sent blurred images back to Earth. However, this initial failure was turned into long-term success.

Why launch a telescope into space?

Ever since the telescope was invented in the early 17th century, astronomers have tried to reduce the distorting effects of the Earth's **atmosphere** on their views of space. They have built observatories on high mountains and, during the 20th century, ground-based telescopes made great advances. The American astronomer Edwin Hubble used giant telescopes to study faraway galaxies. They helped him explain the size and structure of the universe. Space scientists eventually realized that the best way to improve the telescope was to put it beyond Earth's atmosphere. They named the world's first space telescope after Edwin Hubble and sent it into orbit 569 kilometres (353 miles) above the surface of Earth.

Looking beyond the atmosphere

The first person to suggest sending a telescope into space was the German physicist Hermann Oberth. He was followed by the US physicist Lyman Spitzer, who helped create an Orbiting Astronomical Observatory in 1966. Nine years later, the US National Aeronautics and Space Administration (NASA) started work with the European Space Agency (ESA) on a space telescope. Development of the HST took 11 years of hard work, and it was scheduled for launch in autumn 1986. Then disaster struck. Space shuttle *Challenger* exploded shortly after take-off on 28 January 1986, killing seven astronauts. All shuttle missions were stopped, and the finished telescope parts were put in storage. Four years later the HST at last blasted off and was launched into orbit by space shuttle *Discovery*.

This is the Hubble Space Telescope in orbit around Earth.

Problem in space

Imagine the disappointment throughout the astronomical world when the first pictures from the HST were blurry. If a problem with the telescope equipment had been discovered before launch, it could have been dealt with quite easily. What could the scientists and engineers do now that the HST was hundreds of kilometres up in space, travelling at 8 kilometres (5 miles) a second? Was the HST doomed to failure?

"Failure is not an option"

"Failure is not an option" has been used as a motto for space exploration. NASA flight director Eugene Kranz is supposed to have said it in 1970 during the *Apollo 13* Moon mission. The spacecraft experienced an explosion in space but returned safely to Earth.

Apparently Kranz never actually said these words, but he liked them so much that he later used them as the title of his autobiography. Many people feel that the saying sums up NASA's attitude. Obviously there have been space failures, including loss of life, but controllers were determined to keep them to a minimum.

Turning failure to success

Engineers could tell from the faulty images that the cause of the problem was the main light-gathering mirror. It had a flaw called "spherical aberration", which meant that it was very slightly out of shape. One part of the mirror was out by about one-fiftieth the thickness of a human hair. This caused some light to bounce off at slightly the wrong angle, causing a blur. The scientists worked out a solution using a series of small mirrors to correct the flaw. These could be placed on top of the main mirror by astronauts sent up to the HST in a shuttle. The scientists and astronauts spent 11 months training for this mission.

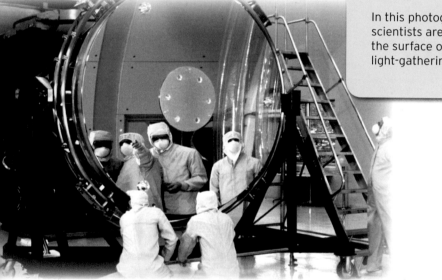

In this photograph, scientists are examining the surface of Hubble's light-gathering mirror.

Space repair

In December 1993 space shuttle *Endeavor* carried a crew of seven astronauts up to the HST. Working from the shuttle payload bay and outside the spacecraft, the astronauts fixed the mirror, and corrected other instruments. They were finished seven days later, and NASA soon released the first new images. They were clear and sharp. The repairs were a complete success.

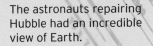

WIN!

The astronauts repairing Hubble had an incredible view of Earth.

Success with infrared?

NASA and the ESA are working on a successor to Hubble. The James Webb Space Telescope will detect **infrared** radiation instead of visible light. This will give it the ability to see even further into the distant universe. It is intended for launch in 2014 and will orbit the Sun. The telescope's main mirror will be 6.5 metres (21 feet) across (nearly three times bigger than the Hubble mirror). It will be made of 18 folded, gold-coated segments, which are designed to unfold in space – an added challenge!

What was learned?

It was discovered that the curve of the mirror had been wrongly measured by an instrument called a null corrector, which itself had a slight fault. Because of this fault, the corrector told the technicians that the mirror was perfect. In future, back-up correctors would be used and all the correctors would be checked and double-checked. The HST was a very good idea, but it was so new and specialized that it had to be manufactured perfectly, with every single part checked extremely carefully. The engineers had been less than perfect in their quality control, which was a big lesson for the future.

Timeline

3000 BC	Cement is invented in Egypt
AD 105	Chinese palace attendant Cai Lun invents paper
1608	Dutch optician Hans Lippershey invents the telescope
1824	British bricklayer William Aspdin makes the first Portland cement
1837	US inventor Samuel Morse develops the **telegraph**
1869	Thomas Edison fails to interest people in his vote recorder
1876	Scottish-born US inventor Alexander Graham Bell develops the telephone
1877	Thomas Edison invents the **phonograph**
1879	Thomas Edison develops a long-lasting electric light bulb that can be used in the home
1888	French scientist Étienne-Jules Marey develops a motion-picture camera
1894	Thomas Edison and William Dickson create their Kinetoscope
1895	US businessman King Camp Gillette invents the safety razor
1896	Italian electrical engineer Guglielmo Marconi invents wireless telegraphy (radio)
1900	Samuel Bligh **patents** his dry shaving device
1904	Christian Hülsmeyer demonstrates the Telemobiloscope
1928	US businessman Jacob Schick develops the electric shaver
1936	Scottish engineer Robert Watson-Watt rediscovers **radar**

1947	US scientist Edwin Land's Polaroid instant camera is introduced
1948	US electrical engineer Peter Goldmark develops the long-playing (LP) record
1956	US engineers Charles Ginsberg and others develop the first videotape recorder
1960	US physicist Theodore Maiman demonstrates the first **laser**. Jack Cardiff makes a Smell-O-Vision film.
1964	AT&T launches its Picturephone
1966	Scott Paper Company makes paper dresses
1971	Sony releases a videocassette recorder
1972	Electronics company Philips launches its videodisc
1975	US electrical engineer Steven Sasson invents the digital camera
1977	Bell Laboratories develop a cellular mobile phone. Polaroid develops Polavision.
1983	Sony releases a camcorder (portable video camera and recorder)
1990	British scientist Tim Berners-Lee develops the World Wide Web. The Hubble Space Telescope is launched.
1996	Toshiba launches the DVD in Japan
1999	Sony launches its AIBO canine robot
2000	Honda launches its ASIMO humanoid robot
2003	Internet fridges are available in shops
2009	The film *Avatar* is released, offering a new kind of 3-D experience
2010	Apple Inc. launches its iPad, a small tablet computer

Glossary

Allies countries (the United Kingdom, United States, USSR, and others) that fought the Axis powers (Germany, Italy, Japan, and others) during World War II

astronomical to do with astronomy (the scientific study of stars, planets, and the universe)

atmosphere air around Earth, or, generally, the gas around any planet or moon

automaton (*plural* **automata**) machine with a power source, that can carry out actions on its own

collaborator someone who works with another person to achieve something

consumerism attitude that it is good to acquire material goods; the system that encourages this

disposable designed to be thrown away after use

enterprise willingness to put effort into new ventures; also a new venture such as a business or company

flammable describing something that catches fire easily

hippie person (especially in the 1960s) who went against conventional values and believed in universal love and peace

humanoid creature or invention that looks like a human being

hygiene cleanliness that helps prevent diseases and infections

Industrial Revolution when Britain and other countries were transformed from agricultural into industrial nations in the 18th and 19th centuries

infrared type of ray similar to light, but which is invisible to the human eye

laser device that produces a beam of intense, pure light of only one colour

legislature government body that makes laws

market existing or potential demand for products; also, the group of people who buy a particular kind of product

patent exclusive right of an inventor to make and sell an invention

phonograph machine, also called a gramophone or record player, that reproduces sounds from discs

prototype first example of a new invention

radar Radio Detection and Ranging, an electronic system for detecting ships and aircraft by bouncing radio waves off them and receiving the reflections. Radar also shows the direction and speed of ships and aircraft.

science fiction story or film based on future scientific advances and often involving space or time travel

Speaker officer at the head of a legislature or similar body

synthetic made with artificial rather than natural materials

telegraph method of long-distance communication using electrical codes

Find out more

Books

101 Things You Wish You'd Invented... and Some You Wish No One Had, Richard Horne and Tracey Turner (Walker, 2008)

Great Inventions of the 20th Century, Peter Jedicke (Chelsea House, 2007)

Outrageous Inventions, John Townsend (Raintree, 2007)

Ten Inventors Who Changed the World, Clive Gifford (Kingfisher, 2009)

Thomas Edison, Charles Pederson (Abdo, 2007)

Websites

www.ukspaceagency.bis.gov.uk/default.aspx
The UK Space Agency website has lots of information about international space missions, satellite technology, and the United Kingdom's role in space exploration.

www.americaslibrary.gov/aa/edison/aa_edison_subj.html
Find out more about Thomas Edison's inventions, including the ones that failed.

www.radarworld.org/huelsmeyer.html
Read about Christian Hülsmeyer on this website, which also has links to other inventors involved in the history of radar.

http://hubblesite.org
NASA's site on the Hubble Space Telescope includes a link to a page showing you where the HST is in orbit right now.

Further research

There are many different topics related to failed and successful inventions and gadgets. Here are some ideas to research:

- A patent is "a document which grants for a set period the sole right to make, use, or sell some process, invention, or commodity" (*Oxford English Dictionary*). Patents were first issued in the Republic of Venice in 1474, in England in 1623, and in the United States in 1790. They have always been extremely important to inventors, since they protect their interests. Many successful patents have covered totally failed inventions. You can use Google to search for interesting patents: visit www.google.com/patents.

- The history of space travel is full of new inventions, and these have produced many highs and lows. Rivalry between the United States and the USSR, known as the Space Race, pushed things forward at a fast rate. Sometimes the first attempt was a failure, as happened with the Hubble Space Telescope, but later developments put things right. There are many books and websites that list space triumphs and disasters.

- Christian Hülsmeyer (see pages 34–37) was just one of the many scientists involved in the history of radar. Try to find out about some of the others. During the 1930s, as World War II approached, various countries tried to beat each other to the goal of having a working radar system. Although it had started with commercial shipping, radar became a military tool during the war years. Today, radar is still used in the military, as well as for navigation in shipping, flying, and on roads.

Index

3-D movies 10

AIBO robotic dog 21
aromatherapy 12
ASIMO robot 19, 20
audio toys 14–17
automata 18

batteries 17, 32
Bell, Alexander Graham 4
Betamax 44
Bligh, Samuel 30–32

canine robots 21
Challenger space shuttle
  47
compact discs (CDs) 43
concrete buildings 6, 7
concrete furniture 6–7

Dickson, William 17
digital cameras 45
digital movies 12
digital recorders 44
Discovery space shuttle 47
disposable clothing 22–25
DVDs 43, 44

Edison, Thomas 4, 5, 6–7,
  14, 16, 17, 26–28
electric clothing 25
electric shavers 32, 33
electronic voting systems
  28, 29
European Space Agency
  (ESA) 46, 49

filibustering 27
film projection 17
fire alarm systems 6
fridges 38–41

Gillette, King Camp 30, 32
gramophone records 14

Hertz, Heinrich 34
hippies 24
Honda Motor Company
  18–19, 20
household robots 18, 20
Hubble, Edwin 46

Hubble Space Telescope
  46–49
Hülsmeyer, Christian
  34–36, 37

Industrial Revolution 4
infrared radiation 49
Internet fridge 38–41
iSmell Personal Scent
  Synthesizer 12

James Webb Space
  Telescope 49

Kinetophone 17
Kinetoscope 17
Kranz, Eugene 47
Kühnold, Rudolf 36

lasers 42
Lasseter, John 17
Laube, Hans 11
Leonardo da Vinci 18
light bulbs 4

microchips 16–17
microwave ovens 39
mobile phones 9, 45

nappies 24
National Aeronautics and
  Space Administration
  (NASA) 46, 47, 48, 49

Oberth, Hermann 46
Odorama 13
Orbiting Astronomical
  Laboratory 46
over-engineering 40

paper clothing 22–25
paper underwear 22, 24
paperless office 41
patents 4, 5, 26, 27, 31,
  36, 55
phonographs 4, 6, 14
Picturephone 8–9
Polaroid 45
Polavision 45
prototypes 27

radar 34–35, 36–37, 55
radio detection-finding
  (RDF) 36, 37
Roberts, Dewitt C. 27
robotics 18–21

safety razors 30, 32, 33
Scent of Mystery (film) 10,
  11–12
Schick, Jacob 32
Scott Paper Company
  22–23
shaving devices 30–33
Shockey, Willis G. 32
smart kitchen appliances
  38–41
smell technology 10–13
Smell-O-Vision 10–12
Sony Corporation 21, 44
spherical aberration 48
Spitzer, Lyman 46

talking dolls 14–17
telegraphic printers 6
Telemobiloscope 34–36, 37
telephones 4, 8–9, 45
touch-screen shopping 41

UMTS technology 9

video cameras 45
Video Home System (VHS)
  44
videocassette recorders
  (VCRs) 44, 45
videocassettes 42, 43
videodiscs 42–45
videophones 8–9
vote recorders 26–29

Watson-Watt, Robert 36, 37
webcams 9